THE BLOCK

The Block
One Block in the South Bronx, 1940s - 1980s

This book was published and printed
thanks to the support of the
New York University Silver School of Social Work

Book design by Kate Hogan

Philip Coltoff
Library of Congress Control Number: 2014911206
Copyright © 2014 by Philip Coltoff
Published in 2014

Printed in the United States

ISBN 978-0-9904831-0-6

2 4 6 8 10 9 7 5 3 1

NYU | SILVER SCHOOL OF SOCIAL WORK

To MAMIE –
an ever helpful
friend and Hastings
Compatriot.
Thanks for your
assistance –
Phil

THE BLOCK

ONE BLOCK IN THE SOUTH BRONX, 1940s - 1980s

By Philip Coltoff

NYU SILVER SCHOOL OF SOCIAL WORK

Other Books by Philip Coltoff

Preventing Child Maltreatment – Begin with the Parent,
coauthored with Allan Luks

The Challenge of Change: Leadership Strategies for
Not-for-Profit Executives and Boards

The Crusade for Children:
The Children's Aid Society's Early Years to Present

At the Crossroads: Not-for-Profit Leadership Strategies

*To the thousands who have lived on the block over
these many years: the parents, the boys, the girls, the new
immigrants, the old-timers. All of them, and those who
reside on Crotona Park East today, constitute a unique
social family and band of brothers.*

CONTENTS

FOREWORD

The *Block* reads like a novel, describing the lives of its inhabitants—the immigrant culture, the peer relationships, and the experiences of the families, especially the youth. I found it interesting, informative and thought provoking. In many ways it is a social history of the period from the 1940s to the 1970s and of the geo-social culture of both the neighborhood and the borough. In reading the book, I began to see that this block was a microcosm of many other blocks, not only in New York City but in urban America. Those of us who grew up in cities, in families that were struggling to make ends meet and adjust to a rapidly changing environment, had similar experiences that reflected our own "growing up." What were our families like? How did they support us? Were cultural and social values transmitted to their children, or was there what sociologists define as "culture conflict" or "lag"? What were our friends like and how were we influenced by the peer group we were part of? *The Block* speaks to the issues that so many of us faced.

In social work today there is a growing understanding of the psycho/social effects on personality and human behavior. We know much more than ever before about the functions of biology, especially brain development. Our deepened understanding of mental issues has enabled our teaching to advance to new and higher levels. That is good and of great benefit to students in our graduate schools and ultimately, to the organizations and clients that they will serve. In recent years, our concentration on the behavioral has limited our appreciation of the environmental, the cultural, and the social. This book helps get us back to understanding that part of human growth and development is the environment where we began, how we learned our self-perception and self-confidence, and the roles we played in groups. Group-work and community organization, two central facets of social work practice, are reflected and described in this book.

I thank Phil for sharing his recollections and experiences as he reflected on his own development—but more importantly, how that experience translates today into cause, social justice, and social action. Communities throughout America are still experiencing difficulty in translating the American way to their lives and struggling for equality and justice. You will enjoy this book, and I believe you will see its application to today's world.

Lynn Videka

Professor and Dean

NYU Silver School of Social Work

PREFACE

The Block is a book that I've always wanted to write. It is about a block in the South Bronx that is one example of many others in urban America. This block, with all its unique qualities, contributed to who I am; but more importantly it had an impact on all its residents, especially its youth.

With all its special physical characteristics, working-class culture, friendships, conflicts, demographics, and responses to an ever-changing social environment, the "block" was an ecosystem unto itself. The people, families, parents, and children who lived there were part of a system; and, consciously or not, they were being shaped by their experiences, their interactions with one another, and their interface with their environment. The block was a social milieu that became a stepping stone especially for its young people and established the foundation for their future development. The power of the environment and the connections between people forged an alliance that for many, determined future course. The love, the peer connection, the cultural experience, the sense of safety and security, the feelings of accomplishment, and being part of a group sustained many who lived in that environment.

I believe my description of the period between the 1940s and 1970s has relevance to today's urban environment. The 21st century immigrants are Asian, Central American, Mexican, and Middle Eastern; they share in many important ways the experiences of the Jewish, Italian, and Puerto Rican newcomers of earlier decades. Sadly, the current African American experience is much the same as it was decades ago. While significant societal changes in upward mobility have occurred, African American families and especially African American youth, remain far behind the white population economically, educationally, and socially. The experience of growing up, of group solidarity and political organization within the context of inequality in America, transcends time and space. The block is a small piece of this larger universe, but it allows us to look at what occurred, what is occurring, and what is likely to be our near-term future with respect to social development, mobility, and personal choice. This book, I trust, will be more than a social commentary and anecdotal review of a time past, but rather a portrait that is not limited by time.

While I was a child who grew up on the block, my adult view is through the lens of a social worker, social engineer, and teacher. We are indeed a product of our environment and our unique makeup, and we need to understand both components.

ACKNOWLEDGEMENTS

Very few books are written singularly by the author. There is always help, guidance, and assistance. Such is certainly the case with this book. A sincere thank-you to Lynn Videka, dean and professor of NYU Silver School of Social Work, who both authored the foreword and made time available to review the manuscript, made many valuable suggestions, and arranged for the book to be printed and published. An extended thank-you to Howard Aibel, who, together with his late wife, made possible my visiting professorship at the School by establishing the Katherine W. and Howard Aibel Chair. Jack Rosenthal, president emeritus of the *NYTimes* Company Foundation, reviewed the manuscript and made many valuable suggestions, as did

ACKNOWLEDGEMENTS

Dr. Gary Rosenberg (the Edith J. Baerwald Professor of Community and Preventive Medicine, Mount Sinai School of Medicine), and Dr. James Blackburn (professor at the Hunter College School of Social Work). An extended thank-you to Jane Kim, a graduate of NYU, who served as both my work-study student and assistant in the writing of *The Block*.

I also acknowledge the assistance of Elizabeth Jenkins, Associate Director of Communications at NYU Silver School of Social Work and her able associate, Kate Hogan, who was instrumental in the design of the book. The assistance of Meg Storey and Ann Webre in editing *The Block* was greatly appreciated.

Without the enthusiastic engagement of former block residents who discussed their recollections with me (their remarks can be found in the final chapter "Recollections in Their Own Words"), especially Gerald Harris, Louise Patalano Wszulkowski, Peter Lerner, and Anthony Scotti, who took the time to write their anecdotes, this book would not have the same meaning to me and to them.

A heartfelt and most sincere thank you to Lynn Harman, my wife, who has always served as my main supporter, confidant, and critic, and who was also the designated photographer. Lynn reviewed the manuscript so often that, after a time, she actually thought she wrote the book.

All of the above are dear colleagues and friends.

INTRODUCTION

The *Block* is a series of chapters about growing up in the Bronx in the 1940s, '50s, '60s, and '70s. It is not just individual reflections, but rather a taste of what was a very important period of change in America post-WWII: increased immigration, diversifying neighborhoods, McCarthyism, and the beginning of the Civil Rights Movement.

The chapters include the time from adolescence through young adulthood and discuss the processes, discoveries, and burdens associated with second- and third-generation children born to immigrant parents.

Back then, the Bronx was a polyglot of populations, including large numbers of immigrant Jews. It was a respite from the teeming streets of the Lower East Side. At the turn of the twentieth century, the Bronx was largely farmland, viewed by many of its newer residents as their Shangri-La. In the post-WWII era, black families were referred to positively as "Negroes." They began to populate the Bronx, coming not only from the South but also from Harlem. The density of the population in Harlem and the lack of affordable housing made the South Bronx more attractive. The great influx of Puerto Rican families also found the Bronx to be less congested than the "barrio" in East Harlem and the extreme poverty that existed in Puerto Rico.

Growing up in this tight, family-oriented, ethnically and racially diverse era was a great exercise in learning and in finding out about yourself, your family, and your place in society.

Chapter 1:
THE BLOCK

In the 1940s the block in the Bronx was much more than a street or even a home. It was your total environment. People left the block to go to work, to school, to shop, and at times, to be entertained. But they always returned to the place they knew, where they were known and felt safe and mostly secure. The block that I am referring to was and is the very last block of a modest five-block stretch of Crotona Park East between Wilkins and Prospect Avenues in the South Bronx.

In the eyes of those who lived there, this block was unique and different from all the others. It had its own shape and contour. There were fire escapes replete with plants, mops, tricycles, and, at times, washed sheets that often signaled a bed wetter in the family. Everything about the block was familiar, from the produce store on the corner to the local butcher shop next door, from the curvature of the buildings as they proceeded in a row toward Prospect Avenue to the distinctive markings on the benches.

The block had a different feel in each season of the year. In summer, people sat on the benches, stickball players played in the street, and others would sit on the stoops to have conversations and political debates. Young children with parents might be lined up waiting to order ice cream from the Bungalow Bar or the Eskimo Pie trucks. Teenagers might be throwing baseballs around in the field or playing "land" with penknives. In winter it was cold and empty outside. Instead, glowing lights from the windows and smoke belching from the chimneys of coal-burning central ovens signaled the life indoors. The block was also host to famous snowfalls. There was the "Big One" in 1947, over twenty inches of snow, and many smaller storms each winter. Sledding in the park, snowball fighting, making snowmen, and cheering over school closings were the main activities.

In the early spring we were out on the block on the cobblestone street playing catch in freezing weather. During this time the Yankees, the Dodgers, and the Giants would be doing their spring training in Florida, which meant that spring training was also upon us. I remember playing catch with a taped baseball and, in between throws, trying to brush away the snowflakes that were falling. Autumn signaled the highly anticipated football season. Touch football was the primary choice. We played against each other in pickup games. As we got older, we also played other teams from neighboring blocks. The block was our stadium and our home field. We knew every inch of the land and played stickball, punch ball, stoop ball, slap ball, and, of course, football.

The block had its other side, the backyard. The rear of the apartment buildings faced a large open area that looked out on the rear of the buildings on Boston Road. Every apartment had a clothesline and regardless of the season they always seemed full. The backyard also had its own history. During WWII it was cleaned up, appropriately divided and shared with all of the residents who wanted to plant Victory Gardens. Victory Gardens were small vegetable gardens meant to promote self-sustainment. When the days of the Victory Gardens passed, the backyard filled up with debris again. However, the backyard also held our clubhouse, which was built without our parents' or landlord's permission. The clubhouse served us well for small parties and card games. It was also the place to go when playing hooky and later on for making out.

We also had the ability to shimmy up the back fire escapes and detach the stick from the mop heads stored on them. The sticks were our stickball bats while the mop heads were left for the resident. Many a Jewish parent who went to mop her floor, especially for the onset of the Sabbath, would find the mop unaccompanied by its handle. In one section of the backyard, several Orthodox families would construct a little house, or a Succoth, where they had their meals for a period of a week following the high holy days.

The block had its good and its bad times. The good was the happiness, the coming home, the huge, free block party at the conclusion of WWII, the family reunions, and the many confirmations and marriages. The block was also where we learned of the death of young men in the war who were our neighbors. It was where we felt deep sadness for those who were injured and for the despondent parents who could not be consoled by neighbors. The block was the centerpiece of our lives and represented a part of our history that was important and determinative of the rest of our lives.

Teaching Questions:

A. What does a block represent to its youth with respect to a sense of home, safety, acceptance, and security?

B. What happens when one doesn't feel accepted or part of a larger block culture?

C. Do memories contribute to a sense of one's identity?

D. Can "attachment theory" transcend family and/or primary caregiver and be transferred to a larger environment?

E. When we think of "environmental theory" do we view a microsystem as the first step in development?

F. How do kids today think of their blocks?

Selected Readings:

- *Mobilization for Youth* by Richard Cloward and George Brager

- "Understanding Culture and Youth Development" by UNESCO

- "Youth in the Ghetto" by Kenneth Clark, an article from *Haryou-Act: a case study of leadership in the ghetto* by Arthur L. Ellis

- *Truants from Life* by Bruno Bettelheim, published by Free Press Paperback: Introduction and pages 389 - 470

Chapter 2:
THE PEOPLE

The block, in an area that was then called the "East Bronx," was made up mostly of first- and second-generation Jewish families. Most of the families moved uptown to escape the teeming, congested, and unhealthy inner city, called the Lower East Side. The Jewish families came mostly from Eastern European countries, principally Russia, Poland, and Hungary. While Jews predominated, significant numbers of Italian families also lived in the community and on the block. The residents identified clearly with their own cultural and religious groups. Nevertheless, we all got along quite well and in some instances long-lasting friendships developed. The boys and girls continued friendships that transcended religion and ethnicity right through college and beyond. Some of the parents also maintained their friendships and social contacts even after they left the block.

The children, especially the second generation had an even more open and accepting view of each other. Everyone came from working-class families and was expected to do well in school and ultimately become economically better off than their parents. While many parents saw college in the future for their children, others expected their children, especially the boys, to become an active part of the work-a-day world and to add to the family's income. Those families who owned small businesses (the local candy store, grocery, barbershop, etc.) wanted their children to come into the business and relieve their fathers of the heavy and long work schedules common in a seven-days-a-week retail business. All of the kids hung out with each other and became best friends. Parents were very accepting of these connections and invited their children's friends to come for Sunday early dinner (Italian families) or, in a few instances, a Sabbath meal.

Still, the harmonious relationships between families did not mean that everything with respect to religious background went smoothly. One day, several of the Jewish boys invited their Italian friends to register for a two-week free summer camp that they attended, sponsored by the local Jewish community center. The children were extremely excited about going to the same camp. However, the children and their parents were shocked to learn that the Italian boys could enroll only after all the Jewish kids and only if there were spots still available. This was a blow to all the boys and an embarrassment for the parents. It was also the first learning experience for everyone about race, religion, and culture. A note: both the Jewish boys and Italian boys never did attend the same summer camp or even try to enroll in future years. These camps were sponsored by social work organizations, which raises the question, from today's perspective, of how sectarian agencies choose to serve a diverse community.

There were other problems that involved religion. A number of the Italian kids and their families were church-goers, and the position of the Catholic Church in the '50s and '60s was that Jews were responsible for the death of Christ. That teaching had some influence on relationships going forward, particularly among the adults who began to feel somewhat uneasy around this sensitive concern. The boys, and for that matter all those of the younger generation, did not experience this issue in the same way and thought of it only when they overheard their parents' conversation at the dinner table. As we grew older, the relationships remained close. Still, it is interesting to note that most of the young people on the block ended up marrying people of their own religious faith. Somewhere down the line, cultural and religious orientation took precedence. However, there were several interracial and interreligious marriages.

Some residents celebrated the Sabbath, while others went to church on Sundays. Ball playing had to wait until everyone returned home and changed clothes. I can still hear the sound of mothers hanging out of open windows, pleading with their children to come home for dinner or shouting that they were sweating too much from their stickball game or weren't dressed properly on a cold day.

When their pleas failed, some would say, "OK, I'm throwing down a peanut butter and jelly sandwich" or, for some, a smaltz sandwich (chicken fat with sautéed onions).

The Catholic boys on the block (there were no Protestants) seemed to have more fun, especially at holiday times. While both the Jewish and Catholic families were close-knit groups, the Catholic kids got gifts, usually new clothing, at Christmas. Being poor, new corduroy pants or a parka or, for that matter, sneakers were all much-wanted items. Although our clothes were usually clean, they were old and secondhand or even thirdhand. At Christmas, when Tony, or Frankie, or Luciano would come out on the block with something new, it created envy on the part of those who were not so fortunate. The Jewish boys longed to have Christmas so that they, too, could receive nice things and feel a part of the larger scene. At school, we sang Christmas carols and gazed at the Christmas tree just outside the school entrance. Even the local stores (there were no supermarkets) were decorated for Christmas with white cotton balls in their windows, glitter, and an occasional Santa Claus. How we longed to be part of that holiday. Yes, there was Hanukkah, but it didn't compare; and in our eyes it was second rate at best. Christmas Day was like any other day for the Jewish boys, but not for our Catholic friends. They had a big meal, family visits, new toys, and new clothing, and they felt part of "Americana." The holidays were one of our first lessons in feeling like outsiders. The acculturation process was in its very beginning stage.

The people began to change as the '50s, '60s, and '70s rolled around. In the '50s, the Jewish and Italian families welcomed a number of Cuban families who moved to the block. Sometime later, several black families moved in, initially serving as building superintendents ("supers") and later as residents. The neighborhood was changing, and Boston Road across the yard south of Prospect Avenue became an African American neighborhood. The influx of African Americans and Puerto Ricans changed the public school population as well and created a social awareness that had not existed before. Expressions of fear and bias began to emerge more visibly, including the need to "protect the block from newcomers." Many believed the newcomers were trying to infiltrate the block and take their apartments, creating a level of distrust and a sense of false "togetherness." As with so many other neighborhoods, families began to move out, especially after two disastrous city and state planning events—the creation of the Cross Bronx Expressway and the building of Co-op City. Those two major and critical urban-planning fiascos shifted between fifty to seventy-five thousand families from existing stable neighborhoods and began the very rapid deterioration of the South Bronx.

In the early 1970s the urban planner Robert Moses was the chief promoter for the creation of the Cross Bronx Expressway, which now runs throughout the Bronx from the Whitestone Bridge to the entrance to the George Washington Bridge. While the highway was a boon for commerce and allowed for a transportation trucking route with easy access to markets in New Jersey and beyond, the social fabric of the community was greatly affected by the construction of the highway. The Cross Bronx Expressway essentially divided the Bronx and, in some ways, created two boroughs within one. North of the highway, the residents were more affluent; south of the highway, they were poorer, more often minority, and less accomplished.

Psychologically, people felt that the highway was a demilitarized zone between two parts of the Bronx. More importantly the effects of the highway, greatly unanticipated, were to uproot the institutional fabric of what had been the East and South Bronx. Within a short period of time, the working class, mostly those in the garment, printing, and millinery industries, began to look elsewhere for their living arrangements. As people left, so did the institutions that had served them and that had helped to create neighborhood stability, such as the synagogue on Prospect Avenue, the Y on Fulton Avenue, the shopping center on Jennings Street. Churches, temples, community centers, shops, stores, and related businesses eventually closed down. The people on the block changed, not only in coloration but also in culture and background. The block that had once been a vital, dynamic, and inspiring place evolved into what is called a "slum." There was little activity, the kids were gone, the benches were empty; the shoptalk, politics, and summer stickball became a memory.

The public schools changed in composition and academic outcomes. The CBE (Cross Bronx Expressway) created a new social structure between haves and have-nots. The Bronx was never the same again.

Where did people go, particularly those of limited means who were subject to the changing manufacturing status of New York City? The garment industry was on the wane, and people were lucky to even be seasonal employees. The answer was Co-op City, constructed on the site of "Freedom Land Amusement Center." The construction of Co-op City, which housed over forty-five thousand people, permitted a mass exodus of working-class families, mainly those who had previously lived south of the CBE and who were anxious to have better housing and escape the stigma of being poor and associated with the South Bronx. The CBE, combined with the construction of Co-op City, changed both the demographics and the sociology of one of New York's major boroughs.

Teaching Questions:

A. What effect does culture have on personality development?

B. Does "group identity" differentiate economically, socially, and developmentally?

C. How do cultural complexity and diversity influence personality development?

D. How does the block represent identification, assimilation, and cultural pluralism?

E. Does being poor create a sense of distance and retreatist behavior?

F. What constitutes individual identity – family, peer group, or ego ideals?

G. What is the relationship between community, environmental, and urban planning and the economic and social status of residents?

Selected Readings:

- *Five Families* by Oscar Lewis
- *Manchild in the Promised Land* by Claude Brown
- *The Old Neighborhood: What We Lost in the Great Suburban Migration, 1966-1999* by Ray Suarez
- *Doing Good: The Limits of Benevolence* by Willard Gaylin and Ira Glasser
- *Delinquency and Opportunity: A Theory of Delinquent Gangs* by Richard A. Cloward and Lloyd E. Ohlin

Diamond One Ballfield

Diamond One, Phil and young ballplayer

Chapter 3:
THE PARK

Crotona Park made the block different from all others and made life fun for everyone. The neighborhood and the South Bronx consisted of what was called "old law tenements." The buildings built in the early 1900s were almost all made of walk-ups that were considered railroad flats. The railroad flat was a straight walk-through with small bedrooms, a kitchen, a living room, and a bathroom that were off a central corridor that resembled a railroad track. Very few of the buildings had elevators, so those who lived on the fourth or fifth floor (the usual height of a building) had quite a job lugging up baby carriages, strollers, and of course, the daily shopping. The buildings were adjacent to each other meaning they shared a common exterior wall which did not allow for much sunlight or air circulation. Each block had many of these tenements on both sides of the street, housing virtually thousands of people. Although people moved to the Bronx to escape the extreme congestion in lower Manhattan, they found little relief up in the Bronx.

Picture each street: Charlotte Street, Seaberry Place, Longfellow Avenue, Bryant Avenue, Boston Road, and Prospect Avenue, all with buildings side by side from one end of the street to the other, packed with families. But while one side of our street looked very congested, the other side was open; it had acres of grassland, ball fields, benches, sycamore trees, tennis courts, a public swimming pool (Crotona Pool), and even some natural rock formation. It was a joy to feel like the country was right outside our door.

The park was therefore a respite, and we came to treat it as ours. We never forgot how lucky we were, especially when hearing envious remarks from other neighbors about our close proximity. Before the mid-1940s, the park was just an open "parade ground" developed somewhat during the early years of the Franklin Roosevelt (FDR) Administration through the creation of the Works Project Administration (WPA). It was because of the WPA that walkways were paved, trees planted, and benches installed. However, the city government developed the park further a few years later. Wonderful ball fields and pedestrian bleachers were constructed throughout Crotona Park. The ball fields, grass outfields, and new fencing were of professional design. "Parkees" maintained the park thoroughly, cutting the grass and dusting the bases so that on weekends and during the summer months the field was magic. Teams from all over the Bronx had the opportunity to play there. Crowds numbering several thousand would sit on the concrete bleachers to watch the games and root for their favorite team which often represented a school, club, or Y. The Bronx PSAL (Public School Athletic League) played its home games on Diamond One, which was one hundred feet from the block. Crotona Park East had its own team in the league, called the Lenrocks. Other diamonds constructed in other parts of Crotona Park were also quite nice; but none, at least in our view, compared with Diamond One.

The excitement felt by the eight- to twelve-year-old boys when the Lenrocks were playing was contagious. We could not wait to get to the bleachers, to watch our heroes, who, of course, were our older brothers or friends of our families. We would watch one game after the other, often forgetting to go home for lunch. We fantasized about a day when we would wear the Lenrocks' uniform and play on a sunlit field while the crowd rooted for us.

The park was also home to handball players and tennis enthusiasts, whom we considered somewhat strange and different. It also had bocce courts that were frequented by the older Italian men, and an artificial lake called "Indian Lake" with a famous large rock called "Indian Rock." Some children claimed that they had found old arrowheads in the park while digging in the dirt. Indian Lake at one time had rowboats, and around it there was a proclaimed lovers' lane that was frequented by young couples. During the Jewish High Holidays, religious men used Indian Lake to deposit lint from their pant pockets, which represented the throwing away of sins accumulated over the year.

The park was important in so many ways. The little ones had swings, seesaws, and a huge sandbox. Preteens had makeshift punch ball fields and bicycle and roller-skating paths. The teens had handball and modified "pitching in" facilities. (A box representing a plate was placed on the handball wall. Then a mark for a mound was placed on the ground.) We practiced pitching, hitting, and fielding in the facilities all the time. The older folks met on the benches to complain about life, encourage political discussion, and engage in gossip. All of these activities were part of our daily routine, but intensified on weekends, summers, and school holidays.

The park was a paradise for the block residents, safe and secure with its ball fields, rowboats on the Indian Lake, and handball and bocce courts. The older guys would venture into what we called "lovers' lane," where girls from other blocks strolled, waiting to be approached.

However, the climate began to shift as the neighborhood and the block experienced demographic changes. As African American and Latino families moved in on the other side of the park, tensions developed, and it became a dividing line between the eastern and western areas. We learned when to use the park, how to use it, when it was safe, and when it was dangerous. We heard of incidents, occasional beatings or a stabbing; some of the reports were no doubt exaggerated, but others were not. The father of one of the boys was a transit conductor who wore a uniform and worked the night shift. He had to cross the park to pick up his train on schedule. His uniform looked like a policeman's and he occasionally carried a club or baton so that it would appear that he was a cop. He would tell us of some of the incidents that he witnessed in the quick fifteen-minute crossing from Crotona Park to Claremont Parkway.

During WWII, the government set up our section of the park, particularly around the Indian Lake, as a training facility for army troops. We saw soldiers engaged in combat training daily. Many of us saw the troops and felt a sense of protection during that period of uncertainty. Those in the military that had leave were treated as celebrities in the neighborhood. The young adult girls were especially pleased to see these troops, since the draft greatly reduced the number of young men in the neighborhood.

Crotona Park was a haven. It was a place to play games and it provided everyone with a place to breathe fresh air. All of these wonderful activities were connected to this special place in our lives that everyone just referred to as "the park."

Teaching Questions

A. Why is "space" important to one's sense of growth? Is space, such as a park, helpful in reducing social claustrophobia?

B. What is the role of government as a creator of space? What social policies need to be developed for space to be available to inner-city youth?

C. What is the role of sports in the development of social skills and behavior formation? Why are sports so crucial for preteens and teens?

D. Does "open space" create opportunities for intergroup relations and social context on shared "common ground"?

E. What does the park reveal about race relations and segregation in the 1940s?

Selected Readings:

- "The Works Projects Administration, Civilian Conservation Core, and National Youth Administration," published by National Archives Summaries

- *Leadership Is an Art* by Max DePree

- *The Crusade for Children: The Children's Aid Society's Early Years to Present* by Philip Coltoff

Phil at Indian Lake, Crotona Park

Indian Rock, Crotona Park

Chapter 4:
THE BOYS

The Boys were separated into various age groups; a two-year age difference set one group apart from another. The groups rarely interacted in any meaningful way. The group above yours was referred to as the "Big Guys." Each group of guys had its own complex system. The oldest group was made up WWII vets. They returned to the block for a short period of time before they moved on, while their parents and younger siblings remained block residents. Each group in succession had its own role and identity; there were the "Big Guys," the "Big Big Guys," and the "Big Big Big Guys."

My group was made up of fifteen guys who were then split up into several subgroups. The older, more athletic and self-asserting guys named themselves the "Big Five." The next subgroup had the slightly younger guys who were good at sports and respectful of the "Big Five." The next subgroup was made up of "Fringe Guys" who were outside of the group for a variety of reasons. For example, Marvin could be found on the block glued to his transistor radio. Taub tried to be a member of the group but lacked the social skills and status and had strange and different ways. His father was a pest exterminator, and he unfortunately was given the title "killer." He hung around but never tried to identify with a group. (Later on he became a right-winger.) Yussy, a gifted cartoonist, became Ticker's one and only friend and both expressed racist ideas. Another boy, the "Professor," while gifted in electronics, was more into setting off cherry bombs on trolley tracks than being part of the group. Frankie, another block inhabitant, was not very good at sports and wandered off to find kids on other blocks.

The central subgroup, called the Big Five, was the centerpiece of all the activities for this junior high school age group. It formed the core of the sports teams and later on, gained the acceptance of the older Big Guys. Of course, a pecking order developed that was determined by skill, looks, school achievement, and social connection. Tony was clearly the leader of the Big Five. He was great at sports, good-looking, and intelligent. He also had great relationship-building skills. Tony knew how to compliment everyone and include them in games and discussions. Stewie was also bright, a good athlete, and a skillful trumpet player with a wonderful sense of humor. His parents were both deaf from birth and Stewie, rather than being embarrassed by his family situation, taught the rest of us sign language. Luciano, the fourth child of an immigrant Italian family, was not very good at team sports; but he excelled in bicycle riding, roller-skating, and mechanical construction. He always had part-time jobs and was our source for part-time employment. Gerry—smart, focused and poetic—served as the group's mediator and arbitrator (later on he became a gifted attorney and criminal court judge). I was a decent athlete and the most interested in politics and liberal causes. I was not a particularly good student and most likely had an undiagnosed learning disability but was nevertheless an active and full member of the group. Each member brought something unique to the whole and was accepted for his contribution. The Big Five continued an active friendship through high school, and maintained contact through college and for a number of years thereafter.

Of course, issues of a complex nature arose from time to time. Tony would often spend a good part of the summer at a relative's home in Vermont. He would be gone for a month or six weeks. The rest of the group members, aside from a two- or three-week stint at a sleep-away camp, remained on the block and engaged in our usual activities without him. We resented his absence, and felt rejection and a real sense of loss, even though we did not really understand our feelings. In our immaturity, we turned temporarily on the source of our hurt even though we had looked forward to Tony's return and counted the days when he would rejoin us. When he returned from Vermont, we gave him the silent treatment which lasted all of two days before Tony said, "What's the matter with you guys?" And with that it ended. That was the power of our connection and his leadership.

Tony was an exceptional ballplayer, street fighter, and protector; and our own status was enhanced by our friendship. The Big Five enjoyed a level of prestige among our peers on the block largely because of him. Tony was more than just a strong, good athlete, he was also a role model. He made us feel secure and important, giving recognition to us when we did good things, saying that we looked good, expressing a liking for a new coat or pair of pants. On occasion, he would invite us, with his mother's permission, to a big Sunday Italian lunch. In other words, we were emotionally connected to him and he in turn, through his presence and leadership, gave us feedback that made us feel good about ourselves. All of this, of course, was not recognized but it was felt. We all knew it, but did not have the security or the capacity to share these feelings with each other.

Social status was important within the group and on the block. This was determined by how well you did in sports, school, and attracting girls. Physical strength and the ability to fight well were also important. When newcomers came to the block, it was only a matter of time before a challenge fight took place. Some newcomers, sensing the pecking order, attempted to act tough to assert their role. They would either assume a high status position or falter, based on the outcome of the fight. Tony was above the fighting; everyone knew that he was the guy who couldn't be beaten and was already the informally appointed leader. The rest of us had to fight to keep our positions, especially when newcomers joined the group.

I remember clearly one fight that I had with Luciano when he moved to the block. It seemed as though we fought for hours, surrounded by a large group of guys. Fights ended when someone cried or had a bloody nose. Luciano and I had a long, drawn-out draw. But another fight with Ernie, a newcomer, resulted in a clear victory on my part and reestablished my status within the group.

The group also competed and occasionally fought with boys for status from other blocks we knew from school or team sports. Fights took place in the schoolyard or the park with groups of boys and girls cheering on their favorite. Tony, of course, was often our stand-up candidate when fighting against the leader of other block groups. Religion and race sometimes entered into the situations. Each block member had his own ethnic identity: the black kids, the Irish kids, etc. Most of the relationships were harmonious and without incident, but sometimes fights occurred over territorial issues.

The boys, of course, each brought their own unique characteristics and personalities. Dickie, while marginal to the group, became the best pocket-pool player not only on the block but also in the neighborhood. It's likely that he went on to make a living as a pool shark.

Glicksman, a toughie and considered by many a deviant, mainly because he was without group identity, was a few years older than us and quite advanced sexually. He went on to become successful in the garment industry—a big surprise to all of us. We had him in a very different industry—one more secure and with bars in the windows.

Every neighborhood has its share of bullies; Glicksman was the prototype. He picked on those who were younger, more vulnerable, and less able to resist. He was a frightening character, especially since he was known to be unpredictable, and his bullying often had sexual overtones. On occasion, when members of our group were "playing hooky" we would run into Glicksman, either in the park (which was a common place for hooky playing) or on the roof of one of the tenements. When that happened, we regretted not going to school that day. On one or two occasions he lined us up, exposed our penises and judged whose was the biggest and most attractive—not a very pleasant experience. As we matured into midrange adolescence and our bodies developed, Glicksman was still unpredictable and to be avoided but he no longer posed a physical threat to any of us. At one point along the way Tony challenged him to a fight, one that we hoped would forever place Glicksman at a disadvantage. Unfortunately, the results were not what we hoped for, but he never did bother us thereafter. Because Tony lost the fight, witnessed by all of us, it reduced our "hero worship" but did not diminish his social status in our eyes.

Bubby, a nickname his mother used and therefore all of us used, went without a real name for years. It was a bit embarrassing later, when he would be introduced on occasion as "Bubby" or "Bubbola" to girls in the neighborhood.

The tenements all looked the same except for the address numbers etched on the front of the buildings. They shared common exterior walls and therefore, the roofs, called "tar beach" by all of us, were used often in the summer for sunbathing. Between two of the buildings there was a large aperture which we called "the crack." In order to move from one roof to the other we had to straddle the crack. There was always the fear that one of us would slip through and bounce from side to side four stories down. One of the boys, Yussy, wanted to attempt to jump from a roof; fortunately, he was stopped before he could display his skills. The crack later became a sign of growth when we were able to straddle it with ease to get to the next roof.

The crack served another purpose. At street level, we stored our stickball apparatuses in it so they could be pulled out quickly to begin a game of stickball. But sticks, for whatever reason, were illegal back then; and the mean cop who patrolled the block, whom we named "Babyface," took joy in confiscating our sticks and often breaking them in front of us. This was frustrating since it was difficult for us to secure those mop sticks. We had to shimmy up windows to unhook them from the mop heads hanging from residents' windows. Babyface never did learn that our sticks were all stored in the crack.

Profiles of the boys who constituted the Big Five:

Tony: the third son of an Italian American immigrant family. The oldest brother Benny was a WWII vet who served in the navy; Frankie was an excellent athlete and student who became an engineer. Tony, the leader of our group, was a terrific athlete and good student who intuitively knew how to compliment and acknowledge others in the group. While he could josh and joke, he also could say nice things that made the rest of us feel good, like "You look very handsome today," "nice tie," "good haircut," "great catch." His presence and approbation were part of his leadership qualities. Tony was accepted into King's

Point Merchant Marine Academy, graduated and became a successful engineer in the petroleum industry.

Stewie: the second son of parents who were both Jewish and totally deaf. Stewie's older brother, Larry, while a good athlete, was considered by his friends to be difficult and explosive. Stewie's personality was just the opposite—friendly, warm, giving; he was a good student, a good athlete, and a good friend. He taught the rest of the guys sign language so that we could also communicate with his parents. Stewie went on to become a successful businessman in the women's apparel industry.

Gerald: the second of three children in an immigrant Jewish family. His father was the longest-serving conductor in the New York City subway system and his mother a school secretary. Gerald, too, was a good athlete, though a mediocre student until high school, when he excelled academically. He was the most introspective of the group; he would privately write poetry, and only later did we learn of this interest. He was a Phi Beta Kappa and suma cum laude scholar in college and at the top of his class in law school. Gerald became a successful lawyer in private practice, twice leaving his firm to become a public servant, first as the Westchester County attorney and then as a deputy commissioner of the New York City's Administration for Children's services.

Luciano: the fourth of six children in an Italian immigrant family. Luciano, a devoted family member, started working part-time as a newsboy when he was twelve years old and always had part-time jobs to help support his family. He was a good student and friend. Even though he was not a gifted athlete, he was an exceptional roller skater and bicycle rider, skills that he freely offered to teach the other members of the group. He married his childhood sweetheart, received an engineering degree, became a successful engineer, and raised a family.

Philly: the third child of a Jewish immigrant family, a good athlete and perhaps the least achieving in public school. Philly's group membership became somewhat tenuous in his teenage years when he developed an active interest in politics and social causes. He developed friendships with groups outside the block and, to some extent, grew distant from his other boyhood friends. However, the group never rejected him and always accepted his less-than-active involvement. His successful school career developed later in high school and then in college and graduate school. He became a social worker, directed the Children's Aid Society in New York for over twenty-five years, and concluded his career as a visiting professor and executive-in-residence at New York University's Silver School of Social Work and is the author of this and other books.

Teaching Questions

A. What's important to a single-sex peer group?

B. How is group identity developed and formed?

C. What is the power of the group to determine the direction, activity, and purpose of its members?

D. Please identify the types of groups that exist, e.g., social group, task group, action group.

E. How do leaders develop and can leader characteristics be seen early in peer group relations?

F. How is a pecking order formed, and what are its effects on the different constituents?

G. What constitutes group aspirations? How does peer culture influence development?

H. Why is physical strength or prowess so important among boys, especially those in low-income or poor communities?

I. How are group cohesion and a sense of loyalty sustained and maintained?

Selected Readings:

- *The Small Group* by Michael S. Olmstead, published by Smith College/Random House

- *Theories for Direct Social Work Practice* by Joseph Walsh: pages 279 – 289

- *Lessons for Lifeguards: Working with Teens When the Topic is Hope* by Dr. Michael A. Carrera

- *The Challenge of Change: Leadership Strategies for Not-for-Profit Executives and Boards* by Philip Coltoff

- *Growing Up Absurd: Problems of Youth in the Organized Society* by Paul Goodman

Chapter 5:
THE BIG GUYS

Every neighborhood had a pecking order. The "Big Guys" were usually defined by age but also by their talent, educational achievement, strength, and ingenuity. When these qualities were either combined or singularly developed in certain boys, they came together to constitute a very special group called the Big Guys. The Big Guys were at times emulated, and at other times feared. They often set the tone for peer life on the block. They demanded respect, deference, and acknowledgment of their social standing.

There wasn't one set of Big Guys. The Big Guys had their own Big Guys, and the social structure was indeed generational. The oldest Big Guys were in their twenties; after WWII, they were veterans. Through the '40s, '50s, and into the '60s, there was very little mobility; if you lived on the block, you would likely stay on the block or you would move only if your finances and lifestyle (like marriage) allowed you to. Everybody knew everybody else, their extended families, their business, personal economy, and love lives.

The Big Guys were well known to numerous peer groups that followed them. Folklore developed around the oldest Big Guys: where they were in the war, how many Germans they killed, how many planes they shot down and how attractive their girlfriends and, later, their wives were. The folklore continued and was passed down so that fact and fiction became one. Sure, "Pannitz" could have been a world champion fighter, "Mutty" could be a great pitcher for the Cleveland Indians, and "Dickie" was besting Minnesota Fats on a pool table. The younger guys watched the Big Guys play ball, gather on the corner, stroll with their girlfriends in the park and at times, establish a makeshift ring while watching two of the Big Guys fight.

If you were seen by the Big Guys as "cool" for being a good athlete and you paid them homage without speaking often, you could hang out on their fringes and listen to their conversation. When I was thirteen and quite hormonal Billy, a Big Guy who later became a police officer, declared a bold statement to his friends. He said, "I figured it out! The two most important things in life are money and sex!" I couldn't understand at the time why money was so important.

Each group was insular and established its own pecking order. On occasion, a group would allow the younger in-between next-in-line a peek into its social order. This was particularly true if an extra outfielder was needed or if a younger guy had something special to offer, like money or an empty apartment to hang out in when playing hooky while his parents worked.

Everyone wanted to be like the Big Guys. There were some who were nicer and more accepting and treated the little guys in a more generous and kinder way. Some of the Big Guys were meaner and insulting. They might give you an uncomplimentary nickname ("Ichabod" if you were tall and thin, "Meatball" if you were Italian and robust, "Dumbo" if you had big ears, "Stick" if you were razor thin and "Professor" if you engaged in weird science experiments such as creating a firecracker or cherry bomb and placing it under a trolley or bus). The Big Guys could also give a "knobber," which was a knuckle to the back of the head, or a "bung," which was a finger flick to the back of your ear. They also had territorial rights. During the winter, the slight slope in the park was theirs first for sledding. If you had a sled, they might claim it for an hour or allow you to go down the hill only after they jumped on your back and went down with you. They had power and control. The only thing that was good about it was that we were the Big Guys to the kids younger than us. So while we took lots of guff from the older guys, we gave it equally to the younger guys. Our social order served to educate; it passed on the knowledge, folklore, history, and mores that were all part of the block. We gained more prestige in our roles and statuses as we grew older, often the result of our effective understanding of the Big Guy culture.

Many years after most of us left the block and entered adulthood, we occasionally had reunions that would bring the different age groups together. The Big Guys, who had seemed so formidable to us growing up, took on a totally different characteristic when we matured. The three-year difference that was so big when we were ten and thirteen became insignificant. That experience itself was very interesting and required reconciliation in our minds of what the Big Guys were really like in the old days. Suddenly, they seemed shorter, less powerful, less knowledgeable, and less good-looking. We no longer saw them as the Big Guys to be emulated, followed, and intimidated by. Some of the Big Guys actually began to see us as very accomplished and their equals. Role reversals took place since, our group, by and large, went on to higher education more frequently than the older group or, as we called them, the Big Guys.

Teaching Questions

A. Why are the Big Guys so important? What do they represent?

B. Why do young people aspire to identify with older peers? What does acceptance mean to the development of personality?

C. How do the Big Guys validate the younger members? Are the Big Guys important in establishing the social norm and values?

D. What's passed down culturally and how is it integrated?

E. What is the influence of "hero worship" on our development? How does earlier perception influence us even as we mature?

F. As we grew older, the importance of the group diminished. Why do you think that is?

Selected Readings:

- *The Small Group* by Michael S. Olmstead, published by Smith College/Random House
- *Problems of Youth: Transition to Adulthood in a Changing World* by Muzafer Sherif and Carolyn W. Sherif, published by Aldine Publishing Company/Chicago: pages 15 - 36, 89 - 110, 235 - 295
- *Reveille for Radicals* by Saul Alinsky
- *Sex: The Facts, the Acts & Your Feelings* by Michael Carrera

Public School 61

Chapter 6:
THE SCHOOLS

While the block was a unique and complete environment unto itself, the public schools were in many ways an extension of it. My elementary school was three blocks away, the junior high four blocks away and the high school a fifteen-minute walk. The elementary school, P.S. 61, now Community School 61, was where kids from the surrounding blocks merged. Primary friendships still centered on the kids from your block to whom you owed your allegiance and loyalty but "cross-cultural" contact occurred and enlarged our scope and positioning. The kids from my block learned how fortunate we were to have a park across the street from our tenement houses. We'd always assumed that the park was there for us and was part of our environment. The kids from surrounding blocks looked at other tenements that faced their buildings that were separated only by a narrow street. Sunshine was not theirs for the taking, nor was there an opportunity for them to step outside and easily see the sky. They were only two or three blocks away from the park, where there were pastures, ball fields, handball courts, and a city-run swimming pool; but in our world three blocks was like three miles.

Public school was very structured, rigid, and to most of us, uninteresting. You traveled with the same students from one grade to the next with one teacher permanently assigned to each grade. There were many classes in each grade and at times the classes competed with one another for status. Mostly, however, you lived within your classroom. With some exceptions, the teachers were focused on the content, not on the students. You were one of many; they knew our names but not much beyond that. There was blackboard work, homework, and the dreaded calling-you-in-front-of-the-class to provide answers to the teacher's questions. This was often done to embarrass a student whom the teacher thought had misbehaved or not completed his or her homework. Unfortunately, humiliating a student in front of the class was a fairly common form of discipline.

Some teachers would stay after the three o'clock dismissal to help students who needed additional instruction. There were teachers who had the confidence of the parents and, therefore, were comfortable making a home visit and discussing a child's school performance, misbehavior, or absences. They meant well, and while we were struck with fear when seeing a teacher walk up to our block and our building knowing that it was to say that we were not doing well, our parents usually responded positively. The teacher was concerned about us, wanted to share information with the parents and secure their cooperation, all in the interest of improving the student's performance. Sadly, as time went on, home visits disappeared, due to both union regulations and changing neighborhoods, which generated some fear on the part of the teachers. Most teachers started leaving when the three o'clock closing bell rang, anxious to flee not just the school, but the neighborhood.

While corporal punishment was not sanctioned by the board of education or the school's principal, teachers often maintained discipline by use of the "ruler." Some teachers, particularly the old-timers, often kept a twenty-four-inch ruler on their desk visible to everybody and a clear sign that we should behave ourselves. On occasion the ruler was lifted from the desk and found its target. It was not unusual for students to know that certain misbehaviors could result in a quick rap to one's knuckles or rear end. Other teachers did not use physical punishment, but at times harsher means, such as having a misbehaving student wear a triangular "dunce" hat and sit in the back of the room for an indeterminate period. Another punishment was making a student stand in the clothing closet that was found in each room, for a prolonged period of time and be subject, of course, to ridicule by teachers and students. On several occasions, one of the more senior teachers asked a particular student, who happened to be a foster child, to come to the front and put the teacher's rain boots on at the end of the day. This teacher, who was quite obese and perpetually angry, would call on this boy to relieve her of the burden of bending down. To our great surprise, one day, this twelve-year-old announced to her and the class that he would not do that anymore. She was shocked and we were worried about the retribution but also very proud of him. He gained the respect of the entire class and the teacher never again asked him or any other student to put her boots on.

It was no wonder that most students viewed the school as oppressive, scary, and cold. The objective was to get through the day, regardless of what was learned. Fun began after three o'clock. Kids would flock out of school in masses and go home, deposit their books, remove their white shirts and ties (on assembly days), and head for the park. The day for us was just beginning. Ahead of us lay games, races, and team sports. More learning happened after three o'clock than during the school day. We learned from each other, from the older kids and from our environment that surrounded us. Finding buried arrows in the park was the beginning of our understanding of Indian folklore. We learned to boat and fish at Indian Lake. We also learned about astronomy from viewing the planets and the sky as nighttime approached. Our education in many instances was profound in that it redirected our energy and gave us a sense of who we were, what we were doing, how it mattered to others, and how it made us feel.

An example of this sense of accomplishment unrelated to school performance was our actual construction of a "hangout." While the park was always inviting, it was visible to parents and other block residents and did not offer a sense of privacy; it was also quite cold as the weather turned to winter. We decided to build our own clubhouse. To do it, eight or ten of us went to a former swimming pool site along the Bronx River where there had been a fire that closed the pool, but some of the lumber remained untouched by the fire. Whether legal or not, we were able to enter the site, secure the lumber and actually float some of it down the Bronx River to a spot where we could then transport it one mile to our block. From there, we managed to get the lumber through the basements of some of the buildings to the large backyard where tenement clotheslines were the major sign of industry. At one time, during World War II, residents of the tenements surrounding the backyard had small Victory Gardens where they grew vegetables and fruits, but now it was nothing more than a repository for junk. We cleared an area, created a rudimentary foundation, used the lumber to build what was probably a ten-by-fourteen clubhouse, secured junk furniture, and actually installed two windows in the clubhouse. (I do not remember how we secured the glass or installed it.) We built a chimney so that we could heat the clubhouse, a very stupid move. Fortunately, while we did not start a fire, we did create a smokehouse, not only from the fire pit that we built but also due to our incessant smoking of cigarettes. Building the clubhouse was an act of creativity, cooperation and group support; but the consequences reflected the limited foresight of thirteen- and fourteen-year-olds. We were discovered because of the smoke that emanated from the chimney. The clubhouse lasted only several months, during which time we had meetings, listened to music, planned different activities, most of which were never carried out, and generally just had a good time. Once our parents and local supers knew what was going on, the days of the clubhouse were over and our hard work demolished.

The park, the block and the rooftops of the tenements were so much more interesting than school that playing hooky was a more exciting alternative to another boring day. A successful "hooky" required a great deal of planning and ingenuity. Remember, we're talking about ten-, eleven-, and twelve-year-olds. On many of our hooky days we were caught or apprehended by police, truant officers, teachers, parents, or block "lookouts." The successful hookies meant knowing when to play hooky, where to go, what to do, what explanation to give when our parents asked about school, what to do with the books that we had to carry to and from school each day, how to get home at the exact time for lunch and at the end of the school day, and how to make it look normal. More than that, a successful hooky often meant providing a clear explanation of what we "learned" in school that day and providing a student witness who might testify to that fib. It might also require intercepting the mail a day or two later since a postcard was often sent home telling parents of our absence. Retrieving the postcard or, at times, changing an absence on our report card and then changing it back again to its original form required enormous dexterity and risk taking, all of which constituted a "successful hooky." Careful planning, critical thinking, understanding the consequences, and taking the risk were all part of the process. (Of course, there were absolutely outrageous moments, like our playing hooky on an open school day, when parents were invited to come to visit our classes, talk to our teachers, and generally observe our work. They expected to see their child in the classroom, only to learn from the teacher that we just weren't there that day. It was embarrassing for all.) The time spent playing hooky, connecting to others engaged in the same activity, and learning the art of planning and implementation resulted in enormous steps in strategic learning. While we didn't realize this at the time, we were preparing ourselves for independent and critical thinking for the years to come.

Junior high (or "middle school" in today's terms) was a jump forward and not just academically. While Junior

High 98 (Hermann Ridder) was just one block north of the elementary school, it was much more than physical distance. It was newer, seemed enormous, and served a larger geographic area. Children from blocks that were unknown to our little world attended the school. There were big corridors, separate stairways, a one-thousand-seat auditorium and of course, "departmental courses," meaning that you traveled from course to course to different rooms with different teachers for each subject. Most of us initially felt overwhelmed by this new world, but we mastered it soon enough. We enjoyed the sense that we were growing up and being treated differently. Having many teachers also helped and gave a new sense of security because if one teacher didn't like you or if one subject was boring, you could anticipate something better in the next class with the next teacher. We learned to navigate the system and enjoyed a new sense of opportunity to achieve.

Junior high was also one of our first intercultural experiences. While our elementary school in the 1940s and '50s was marginally integrated (whites, African Americans, and Puerto Ricans) the junior high school drew on a larger geographic area and had many more students from different backgrounds and cultures. While the school was still primarily white and Jewish, we had real and continued contact with students of Irish and Italian backgrounds, Latinos other than Puerto Ricans (mostly Cubans), and African Americans. While our primary friends remained, new friendships were established. We also started to become interested in girls. While we had our own "girls group" from the block, the new school provided additional opportunities. Crushes developed, parties at the local Y were scheduled, and more importantly, we had new groups of baseball, basketball, and football teams to play through our expanded relationships. School was less boring; and although it would be a stretch to say it was exciting, we were certainly enlarging our scope and were no longer time-warped within the world centering on our block.

Morris High School, the second-oldest school in the city of New York, was huge and architecturally as stunning as the City College of New York. We started high school in tenth grade. We walked or hitched a ride through an inexpensive bus pass or a free ride by hanging on to the back of the bus. Here was where our world really expanded. All of our friends on the block went to Morris High unless they managed to be accepted into one of the specialized high schools (Bronx Science, Stuyvesant, Brooklyn Tech, or Hunter High). Other than being the largest buildings we ever saw (our trips to Manhattan were indeed rare), the school had several thousand students coming from a large section of the South Bronx, which included Mott Haven, Soundview, and Morrisania. The colors and the backgrounds of the students were the first noticeable changes. Prior to redistricting, Morris was mostly an African American school. So on our block, we were the first white students to attend Morris in decades. Boston Road was a dividing line and the area east and south of that road was, even in the '40s and '50s, populated by African Americans. We entered the school with some trepidation, reinforced by our parent's fear of change and distrust of others who were not of their ethnic group. However, we found the environment so new, different, and exciting that the anxiety dissipated. What occurred in its place was a greatly expanded view of our own little universe. We learned who these new folks were, their backgrounds, cultures, skills, and interests. They learned similarly about us, and remarkably, there was little racial tension. We later realized that we were experiencing "cultural pluralism."

Several of the boys from the block participated in extracurricular activities in sports and music and two became active on the school newspaper, *The Morris Piper*, as the managing editor and sports editor. Our political awareness developed with a clearly progressive bent, and we organized the "Morris High School Peace and Civil Rights Group." One must remember that this was less than ten years after the conclusion of WWII and smack in the middle of the Korean conflict. To many of us war was an anathema, and we were able to organize several dozen students in peace activities. Since Morris was an interracial and integrated school, we also organized a civil rights group that for the first time recruited African American and some Latino students. We had informal talks and lectures, and we participated in some programs run by Saint Augustine's Church, which was several blocks away from the high school and had a very active NAACP Youth Council. In the early 1950s, the most radical civil rights groups were the NAACP and the Urban League, which existed before the emergence of the Congress of Racial Equality (CORE), Student Nonviolent Coordinating Committee (SNCC), and the Southern Christian leadership conference, led by the Rev. Dr. Martin Luther King Jr.

My cousin and I were both ardent New York Yankees baseball fans. The Yankees were among the last teams to racially integrate, late in the 1950s, when they finally brought up Elston Howard from the Negro National Baseball League. Howard, of course, became a great catcher and Hall of Fame nominee. Our group demonstrated outside the stadium on one of their weekend day games, carrying signs that read "Jim Crow must go" and "Integrate the Yankees." There were over one hundred students at this demonstration and at the end of the hour, the police said we had to leave and collected our makeshift signs. It was a successful demonstration. At the conclusion, my cousin and I snuck into the stadium to watch the Yankees play the Red Sox. All in all, it was a pretty fine day.

Our ghetto mentality was permanently put to rest. New friends, classmates, and team members were now in our lives. Attitudes about race, culture, and difference began to shift. We felt like grown-ups and believed in our school. We were proud to be "Morrisites." Thus began our entry into a larger, more complex and more dynamic world.

Teaching Questions

A. What is the role of the school as a social transformer? Is the school viewed as a positive force in a poor community?

B. Is the school an extension of the community, and does it reflect community aspirations and values?

C. Does the school play a significant role in influencing community and family life?

D. Should the school be an "island of safety," removed and distant from community life, or should the school be an extension of community life?

E. What roles do parents play or should they play in school policy?

F. How does the development of the more recent concept of "community schooling" relate to the traditional public school serving low-income students?

G. Should the schools be an environment that encourages integration of racial, ethnic, and national student bodies? Where possible, should schools be districted (legislated) to serve multiethnic student bodies?

H. What role should teachers and school administrators play in the development of sound teaching materials that encourage students to be effective learners and to view the school positively?

I. What meaning and function does the clubhouse serve for the boys?

Selected Readings:

- *Inside Full-Service Community Schools* by Joy G. Dryfoos, published by Josey-Bass Publishers: pages 1 - 99

- *Building a Community School*, Third Edition, by The Children's Aid Society

- *Community Schools in Action: Lessons from a Decade of Practice* by Joy G. Dryfoos, Jane Quinn, Carol Barkin, published by Oxford University Press

- *Social Work Services in Schools* by Paula Allen-Meares

- Manual for Intergroup Relations by John P. Dean, Alex Rosen

Chapter 7:
THE GIRLS

The girls were always on the block, but the boys hardly noticed them at first. When we were preadolescent, our lives centered on sports, having fun, testing our limits, establishing our status, and, as said in an earlier chapter, having successful hookies. We passed the girls on the block, witnessed their interactions with each other, and often teased them by pulling their ponytails or commenting on their looks. They were there, but hardly a part of our lives; they, in turn, had about as much interest in us as we had in them.

Then adolescence, hormones, and physical and mental growth changed everything. The girls became very much noticed. We didn't pull their ponytails anymore; there were too many other things that commanded our interest. No longer was the block a game center or a stickball field; it became a social gathering place. This new round in the life cycle created a new social hierarchy, pecking order, and image makeover. The boys, who previously were ranked by their games and sports abilities, now had to refine their social skills. Pegged pants, pompadours and open collars became not only status symbols but also things that attracted the girls. Bernie, Dickie, and Bubby who had little preadolescent capital, gained much attention after adolescence hit. Now we had other things to worry about. Could we get some more money for clothes and new sneakers? Could we convince our parents to allow the local barber to give us a pompadour or slick back our hair into a "duck's ass"? The girls on the block who had ponytails and wore little print dresses soon became our closest friends and playmates.

As junior high morphed into high school, our group became much more coed. Crushes developed and friendships turned into relationships. Couplings included

Stewie and Louise, Tony and Chickie, Bernie and Harriet, Jerry and Betty, and Philly and Esther. From time to time others broke into the group, and relationships would shift. Friday nights were party nights. We would seek out an apartment with our parents' consent (or otherwise) where a party could be held. The party always had the same kids and more often than not, the same couples. There was talking, dancing, smoking and, as we got older, drinking. The slow close dancing would soon turn into kissing and at times, petting. Most of the contact, if not innocent, was experimental. Together we were learning the fundamentals of psycho-sexual relationships.

Interestingly, the dyad relationships remained fairly constant for a number of years. At Friday night parties, some "switching" would occur experimentally but did not alter the primary relational connection. Stewie and Louise had the longest and most stable relationship. While we were curious about the extent of it and asked Stewie about it, it remained a mystery. We had to deal with our own changing physiology as well as maintain new social contacts. Slow dancing, of course, produced an erection which initially embarrassed us. We would try to hide the occurrence by wearing a tight jock strap which was a silly maneuver that never really worked. As time went on, the jock straps came off and both the girls and boys eventually acknowledged that an erection was healthy and not at all an embarrassment. Of course, the parties then became more interesting as a result of our psychological growth.

There were a few girls on the block who were on the fringe of our group, older than us and quite sexually advanced. While they were accepted as a part of the block, they were seen as different; as we got older, some of them became our "sexual teachers." Because this was unusual and these few girls were out of our social orbit, the events were often talked about in congratulatory terms. "Did you do it?" "Did she offer it to you?" "Was this your first lay?" Sydney, one of the more knowledgeable girls would suggest a walk in the park when it was dark, which often resulted in heavy petting and on several occasions, intercourse. She would often select "the cute boys" or those who had special status. In a strange way, Sydney was our stepping-stone to more advanced sexuality.

As we grew into our high school years, we expanded our social relationships culturally. Other girls from blocks near ours became part of our group. These new connections were an expansion of our own very limited geographic domain. The girls were all in the working class and were of Jewish, Italian, or Latino descent.

In our junior year in high school, seven of us each contributed five dollars which allowed us to rent a small room in the Rockaways on weekends during the summer months. The bed held three; the other four slept on the floor. We spent most of our time on the beach and the boardwalk, where we met other girls. I recall one meeting on the boardwalk with girls from Ocean Parkway in Brooklyn. We didn't know much but we did know that Ocean Parkway was where rich girls lived. We also knew that we lived in a poor, working-class area called the East Bronx. During our conversation and flirtation with these rich girls, they asked us where we lived. Our response was "a few blocks off the Concourse"; everyone knew that the one area in the Bronx that had social status was the Grand Concourse, which resembled the Champs

Elysees. However, we didn't live a few blocks from the Concourse, we were actually several miles to the east. The girls believed that we lived in the richer area and invited us to join them that night for activities. Our world was ever expanding.

Teaching Questions

A. What do we know of the social and sexual development of children? What should be taught during latency to make the transition to adolescence easier?

B. Should schools, social and recreational agencies, and religious organizations encourage more coeducational programs?

C. What are the ways in which we teach sexuality? Are we reluctant and resistant to the notion that children and youth are sexual beings? How can adults develop greater comfort in working with teen sexuality?

D. What is the perception of boys with respect to girls? Have we advanced sufficiently for boys to see girls as more than sexual beings and as equals? How do you think the girls in Chapter 7 viewed the guys?

E. What do we need to do to help girls and boys view themselves as able, creative people whose minds are equal to the development of their bodies?

F. Under what conditions do early heterosexual relationships help in the development of better, more stable, and more lasting adult relationships?

G. Should schools of social work be more active in including adolescent sexuality within the prescribed curriculum?

Selected Readings:

- *Sex: The Facts, the Acts and Your Feelings* by Michael Carrera, published by Crown Publishers
- *Doing Good: The Limits of Benevolence* by Willard Gaylin and Ira Glasser, published by Pantheon Books
- *Childhood and Adolescence: A Psychology of the Growing Person* by L. Joseph Stone, Joseph Church, Otto Klineberg
- *Pregnant and Parenting Adolescents: A Study of Services* by Francine J. Vecchiolla, Penelope L. Maza

Phil in front of his stoop

Chapter 8:
THE STOOP

Each tenement had its own six-by-eight stoop – a small platform at the top of three to six steps that led to a long corridor of railroad apartments. The stoop was more than an entranceway and exit; it was an integral part of the block. In nice weather, each stoop became its own "union square political meeting ground." Residents from the building and others on the block would assemble on the stoop to engage in active discussions about everything from the weather to the kids, world events, local politics and of course, block gossip. At times the gatherings were intergenerational with old folks, adults, and kids occupying the same space for a period of time. Mostly, the stoop gatherings occurred spontaneously, and the types of activities that happened there depended on the age of the group. The adults discussed adult things—shopping, who was ill, who'd lost their job, who was receiving welfare, children, and occasionally, what vacation plans they might have. There was healthy storytelling; and most of the discussions were calm and sociable, although sometimes arguments emerged.

The adults usually gathered in the daytime hours or near sunset in nice weather, and they would bring out chairs or boxes to sit on during these informal discussions. The teens usually occupied the stoops in the evenings and on weekends. Their conversations centered on school, sports, games, activities, and the hatching of plans for the week's adventure, such as hooky. Opportunities for socializing on the stoop were somewhat different from using the park benches. For example, the stoop allowed you to run into your apartment to get some lemonade or candy and bring it out to have a party. The stoop also felt more secure, since each building had its own subculture within the larger culture of the block. But when antagonisms developed in school, boys from other blocks always knew that when they came to the block, either to continue an argument or seek revenge, they would most likely find their target on one of the stoops.

The stoop was host to a game called "stoop ball" that was famous throughout the Bronx and beyond. Because each stoop had between three and six steps leading up to the platform, a great game evolved. With a pink rubber "spaldeen" as the centerpiece, teams were made up of anywhere from five to six kids who would fan out from the sidewalk into the street. The object was to throw the ball against the steps and run the bases, which resembled a mini baseball field. We learned how to hit the "point of the steps" which would create great force, resulting in the ball traveling a considerable distance (up to sixty feet) and often resulted in a home run. If the ball hit between two points in the steps, it often resulted in a groundout or an easy pop out. The games were fierce, and the victors along with the vanquished would often finish the game or a rematch exhausted. Usually by the end of the second game, the residents of the building would yell down, "Enough already. We want to go to sleep!"

Street games were unbelievably inventive. We used what we had, reflecting the working-class nature of our environment. The games rarely required money (unless there was a bet on the stickball game). If the spaldeen rolled down the block and into the sewer, we had a can on a string that we lowered down to catch the ball and hoist it up. There was never a thought that we could get a new ball because twenty-five cents was a lot of money. The ball that was being used had to be retrieved. The sidewalks laid out in concrete were constructed with seams that created "boxes" of cement. Those boxes allowed for a game called "boxball," similar to handball, in which a player "owned" a box and used his hand to hit a ball into the other person's box to prevent it being returned to his box. Girls used the same boxes for a game called "potsy." They would number each box with chalk, throw an object, usually a key into a box, hop from one through ten, pick up the key in the box it had landed in while standing on one foot, go to the end, spin around from box to box and return to the start. Not easy, and the winner felt crowned.

"Kick the can" was another game played by teens. One team kicked an empty food can down the block in relay fashion while trying to avoid the reach of the other team's members, and then kicked it back to the start. In between there was much action, such as blocking opponents, which resulted in many a damaged shin. Interestingly, in today's political world, kick the can is referred to as a way of avoiding a problem by kicking it down the road. We didn't see it that way. Our objective was to get the can past the opponent but then get it back to the start which represented a victory, not avoidance.

"Johnny on the pony" was another game that allowed the physically less active players to serve as the "pillow," not requiring them to leap over other bodies; that way everyone could be involved. Many of the games had variations, and depending on one's age and stage, could be made harder or easier to play. All of the games were played with intensity, but more importantly, they were inventive and represented group thinking.

Teaching Questions:

A. What is the value of games as a social experience?

B. What role does competition play in social development?

C. What role did the meeting ground play and what is missing in today's urban living?

Selected Readings:

- *The Life Model of Social Work Practice* by Alex Gitterman, Carel B. Germain, published by Columbia University Press

- *The Party Game Book* by Margaret E. Mulac, Marian S. Holmes, published by Harper & Brothers

- *The Small Group* by Michael S. Olmstead, published by Smith College/Random House

"Johnny on the Pony"

Chapter 9:
THE IMMIGRANT

Russian, Polish, and Hungarian people of Jewish origin populated the block together with Italian and Cuban first- and second-generation families. (African American families mostly were the buildings' supers; their children participated in block events.) The languages therefore were as diverse as the cooking and culture. Each tenement, comprising these immigrant families was truly a "melting pot." We all got used to the different cooking smells, and after a while, we thought all buildings had those wonderful aromas. The immigrant families, whether from Eastern Europe, the Italian boot, or Cuba, all got along and some became close friends. The adults seemed to understand each other's dialects more than the kids did. English was the spoken language, spiced with references from the old country in Yiddish, Italian, or Spanish—as were the derogatory comments about someone's looks, behavior, or style. After awhile, everyone on the block learned the expressions and references even when they were in a different language. The block was indeed a polyglot, although some might say it resembled a European shtetl. Harmonious relations between these different immigrant groups were most common, even though each group had its unique identity—church or synagogue, holidays, and funerals.

The Jewish kids, of course, invited the Italian and Cuban kids to their bar mitzvahs (bat mitzvahs were not yet celebrated). In turn, the Italian kids would invite the Jewish kids up for a big Sunday spaghetti or macaroni dinner. Most of the residents accepted the different styles of communication, family life, and childhood practices. In this respect, the block and its inhabitants were practicing "cultural pluralism" even though they had no idea what that sociological concept was. The various cultures were an accepted part of life. When kids were playing ball across the street in the park, we all knew that as dusk approached, Mrs. Amore would call from her third-floor window that faced the park and say, "Bubby, come up for supper!" Bubby was her son's nickname. Mrs. Amore was of Jewish-Spanish heritage and didn't care that Bubby would be embarrassed by having to leave the game to respond to her call. Luciano's mom, who was on the fifth floor facing the park, would not call him for supper but rather flip down a meatball sandwich so that he could be nourished while playing Johnny on the pony. The languages, dialects and idiosyncrasies all blended into the social climate of the block. We knew families who argued, drank, and were unemployed but also caring and protective.

The working-class nature of the immigrant block also had a political side. Many of the first-generation European immigrants were political leftists, old socialists, and union members of both the Millinery, Fur and International Ladies Garment Workers Union. Workers' rights were seen as important, and unions were viewed as the forefront in protecting those rights. While the

Daily News and the *Daily Mirror* were standard newspaper reading, so were the *Daily Compass* and even the *Daily Worker*. Political arguments often took place on nice days in the park, on the stoop, or in the local candy store. Everyone knew everyone else's political orientation. The arguments, while fierce, were usually respectful. The 1948 election, in which Harry Truman bested Thomas Dewey, was a big deal that created a big stir. But on the block, the winner was a little known left-winger, Henry Wallace, who was a candidate of the Progressive Party and former Vice President and Secretary of Commerce under President Franklin D. Roosevelt. The left-wing/worker orientation was so accepted that when one friend was asked to lend another friend a dollar to go to the movies with a girl and share popcorn, the response might well be, "You think I'm a capitalist?"

This harmony and classless orientation was fractured when newcomers began to populate the neighborhood. Large numbers of African Americans began to move into tenements that were south and east of Boston Road. Puerto Rican families moved in across the park on

Claremont Avenue in significant numbers. No religious organizations or educational institutions played a significant role in bringing groups together. The old immigrant groups felt that their apartments, stores, parks, and schools were being invaded. Intergroup relations took a turn for the worse. Ethnic and racial prejudice became a fact of daily life. After-school fights between whites, blacks, and Puerto Ricans began to determine status and territory. Stereotypes emerged and fractionalization became a part of normal life: "They want to take our apartments and our park." Unfortunately, there was little understanding of neighborhood change as affected by immigration and migration from the South. Schools did not effectively teach culture, tolerance, and difference. The newcomers were seen as different and, of course, they were: their skin was darker, their style and culture were unfamiliar, and their defensive behavior was often a response to feeling unaccepted. It was only after the intervention of neighborhood settlement houses that racial interactions began to improve.

Teaching Questions

A. How are immigrants viewed today?

B. Do we accept "the newcomer" any differently than we did in the last century?

C. What does cultural pluralism, mean and can the Theory of Change help identify cultural conflict, lag, or integration?

D. What is the role today of the Latino population? What social policy needs to be developed to effectively integrate this ever-growing population?

E. How will our social and political systems change with respect to immigration policy by the year 2020, when minorities will constitute the majority population?

F. Is political power still vested in ethnic and minority configurations?

G. Is there still a melting pot and has there ever been one?

Selected Readings:

- *The Americanization of Emily* by William Bradford Huie
- *Beyond the Melting Pot* by Nathan Glazer, Daniel P. Moynihan, published by Harvard University
- *Rebuilding the Nest: A New Commitment to the American Family* by David Blankenhorn, Steven Bayme, Jean Bethke Elshtain

Chapter 10:
THE WAR YEARS

World War II was a very troubled time for neighborhoods and blocks throughout the country. Our block showed the scars of the war almost immediately. Parts of the block emptied out. Every male between the ages of eighteen to thirty-five who was physically able and did not have dependents to care for was drafted into the armed forces. The good-byes were frequent and painful. Hearing mothers cry as their sons departed for the war was commonplace. The younger children were, of course, very proud of the soldiers, sailors, marines, and coast guard men who lived on the block. We imitated them with makeshift uniforms, tree limbs for rifles, and canteens at our waists, as if drinking water were not in walking distance of our apartments. The war cast a long shadow over the block. Fear, insecurity, stress, and uncertainty prevailed.

While families struggled to maintain normalcy, the radio reports of battles abroad added to the sense of despair. Air raid drills in school were weekly; having to hide under your desk, staying away from windows, and having the equivalent of "dog tags" were constant reminders that things were indeed different. Every block had appointed air raid warden citizens—almost always men—who made sure all lights were out during a drill, patrolled the block and made sure that the few automobiles had blackout headlights. While the air raid drills were exciting to the kids, they were taken very seriously by adults. Most grown-ups were aware of the blitz occurring in London. Many thought that would be our fate as well. When a formation of planes was heard and seen overhead, fear gripped the block's inhabitants until a knowledgeable person would say, "Oh, they're ours. P47s."

War reminders abounded. Miniature American flags were placed in apartment windows. Two stars or three stars were placed on the flag if two or three family members were serving in the armed forces. When a gold star was hanging on the flag it signaled that a member of the family had been killed in action. Blue stars signaled someone in the military service. Such flags existed on our block and many others throughout the neighborhood. A local store displayed photos of soldiers, sailors, and marines from the neighborhood who were killed in action. Memorial services in churches and synagogues were regular occurrences. One of the more exciting aspects of the war was that our park was taken over in part as a military base. Tents were set up and military drills were routine. The younger kids were not allowed to enter that section of the park but we would anxiously wait for the end of the day, when the soldiers were allowed to walk into the neighborhood. We would be there to greet them and salute. They often saluted back or placed their army caps on our heads for a moment. It was a great joy. Occasionally, a captain or a major strolled through the block, and we would treat the officer like a hero. We all knew the insignias, the badge and rank identifications; and we collected bubblegum cards that had pictures of American planes, ships, and tanks.

Daily news reports, thick letters, and an occasional package that held a German or Japanese helmet sent from overseas were part of block life. The games that we played were "army games." Old games were replaced with new names, such as "three feet to Germany," which was a game of tag but centered on how fast we could cross the street without being tagged by a "German officer." If we reached the other side, we were closer to capturing Germany and ending the war. Another game, called "land," was played with penknives that were flipped to a grassy area. A "cut" was made when the blade landed marking how much "land" we had captured from the Germans. We held marches and campouts that resembled what we believed to be military training. We would "commandeer" potatoes, which were "borrowed" from the local grocery store, and roast them in an open fire we would make on a rocky area in the park. The potato was called a "mickey"; and while the outside was pure charcoal, the inside was delicious. Somehow, we believed that this was a soldier-like activity.

The atmosphere was heavily charged with fear, which often resulted in derogatory statements about "Krauts" and "Japs." They were the enemy, and Americans of German background were treated with suspicion in the neighborhood. Fewer Japanese families were visible in our neighborhood; but all Asians, including those who ran the local laundry, were referred to as Japs. Older folks needed to remind younger ones that the Chinese, Filipinos, and Koreans were all Asians and many of them were on America's side. The antagonism toward those that were the "Axis" (the Germans and Japanese) lasted for some time. When a number of the soldiers who lived on the block returned home after the war with some German and Japanese war brides, they were initially viewed with suspicion, if not distrust. It took a long time for things to return to normal, for fear to disappear, and for a sense of peace to return.

One of the great moments was the enormous "block party" that was organized by the elders for the returning veterans. The candy store provided free soda, ice cream, cookies, and candy; the local butcher contributed hamburgers and hot dogs, which were cooked on makeshift grills up and down the block. There were banners, music, dancing, and general good cheer. It was a great moment to remember, one that I'm sure the twelve hundred plus people who resided on the block in those twelve tenement buildings will never forget.

Teaching Questions

A. What are the effects of war on children? What scarring occurs?

B. How do we confront fear as an immobilizing force?

C. Do war and other acts of violence create greater instability and individual aggression?

D. Does a warlike atmosphere contribute to the ever-growing presence of weapons in poor communities?

E. How do we control acts of social intimidation?

F. How should social work help to humanize an environment that encourages fear and conflict?

Selected Readings:

- "Aggression and Personality," an article in *Theories of Direct Social Work Practice* by Joseph Walsh: pages 29 - 43

- *Delinquency and Opportunity: A Theory of Delinquent Gangs* by Richard A. Cloward and Lloyd E. Ohlin, published by A Free Press

- *Giving in America: Toward a Stronger Voluntary Sector* by Commission on Private Philanthropy and Public Needs, Filer: John H.

- *Company K* by William March

Chapter 11:
AFTER THE WAR YEARS

The war ended, peace was restored, and soldiers returned home to waiting families. Other than the loss of lives followed by a period of grieving, life resembled what it had been like prior to the war years. The names of the games changed back to "kick the can," "pitching in," "stoop ball," and "ring-a-leave-e-o." The servicemen, who returned older and wiser, re-formed their old social club named "Lenrocks." The Lenrocks had a baseball team with wonderful uniforms and owned a clubhouse. Younger kids were not allowed to enter or even approach the club. That was their place for card games, drinking, and dancing. The Big Guys were still the Big Guys, although all of us had stepped up at least one generation.

Adults on the block still mourned the loss of Franklin Delano Roosevelt. His death caused considerable insecurity about the future and a sense of being without a leader. After the president's death, the most popular national figure was his wife, Eleanor Roosevelt. She epitomized what America stood for as well as our dreams and aspirations. She was a protector of working people. Some of the consequences of the after-war years were problems that many did not anticipate. Older men, who were not in the service, had very good jobs that paid very well during the war years, especially if they were in the defense industry. Their salaries, as compared to their prewar jobs, doubled and tripled. They were able to save and anticipate a much better life. However, after the war those jobs disappeared; and many of the men and some of the women had to scramble again to drive a taxi, sell local newspapers or eggs, or try to get a civil service job in the post office. The standard of living dipped, although people felt greatly relieved that the struggle and fear generated in the war years were over.

However, the political situation was unstable after Roosevelt's death. The Cold War soon replaced the hot war, and the political divisions between left and right were accentuated. The Soviet Union, which had been our great ally during the war against Germany, now became our archenemy. Signs against "Communists" could be found everywhere. Red-baiting (finding or locating those that were left-wing and referred to as "pinkos") became the order of the day, and the blacklist in Hollywood was in effect (actors and writers who were considered left-wing or progressive were barred by the Hollywood studios). Anybody caught reading the *Daily Worker* (the Communist Party newspaper) would not only be subject to ridicule but might also lose his or her job, as did many school teachers and other public service workers. McCarthyism was the political rule of the day. If you were a true American, you needed to be anti-Soviet, and in some ways, anti-working class. This national atmosphere penetrated the families on the block. While most could be considered liberal, working class, and left-leaning, others—out of belief or fear—began to take a more right-wing position. McCarthyism had a large social impact on families, friendships, and social relationships on the block. "Are you a Communist, a Communist sympathizer, a union member, or a Russian?" Or "Who do you vote for?" These questions were often asked. Some of the residents tried to outdo others with respect to being "American" and showing belief in our system and our flag. It was indeed a difficult time, and a level of division existed that had not been seen or felt before. Apprehension, fear, and reprisal were all real factors that were felt in people's lives, almost on a daily basis. The anti-Communist hysteria affected all, with the young people being very aware of who was "left-leaning" and who was "pro-American." The situation was even more complicated for those whose families were under attack because of their union affiliation or socialist orientation.

The years after the war were tumultuous. While our economy and our population grew, great shortages existed, particularly in housing. The war years had created rationing and a "meatless Tuesday." Rationing did not end immediately after 1945. Black marketing took hold, along with a rather robust underground economy. Those who could get you a portable battery-driven radio, a car, and a "spaldeen" were very popular. Those people who could suggest an apartment for a vet who was just married were sought after. In many cases, the vets returning home shared a small apartment with three generations. The GI Bill enabled millions of returned vets to have a free college education. The bill spurred one of the major institutional changes in America. Scores of returning servicemen who otherwise would not have been able to afford or even consider a college education took full advantage of the program. Many teens sought part-time jobs (newsboy and delivery jobs) to help augment family income. Despite the political issues, America was indeed moving forward, and life was getting much better.

By the end of the 1950s, McCarthyism was defeated, and red-baiting ceased. Political stability returned. The block was normalized, but interesting new habitants started to arrive. Many Jewish and Italian families had saved enough to move to the suburbs. In the late '60s and '70s, their old apartments became occupied by black or Latino families. After half a century, the character and quality of the block began to change. The residents of the block were moving more to a middle-class status and losing their working-class character. Many of the families found new homes in the North Bronx and some in the suburbs. Interestingly, the youth, who by then were quite mobile, stayed actively in contact with each other.

Teaching Questions

A. How do we build bridges to resolve community conflicts? Can conflict resolution programs help to overcome stress and isolation?

B. How does post-traumatic stress disorder, "PTSD," affect both those who were engaged in combat and those on the home front—especially youth?

C. Can group therapies be an effective method in coping with PTSD, and what has been the experience after conflicts have ended?

D. How does early trauma create greater vulnerability to larger social disorder?

E. What is the role of social work as an instrument for change?

Selected Readings:

- *Gentlemen's Agreement* a film directed by Elia Kazan (1947)
- *On a Note of Triumph* by Norman Corwin
- *Childhood and Adolescence: A Psychology of the Growing Person* by by L. Joseph Stone, Joseph Church, Otto Klineberg
- *Solomon's Sword* by Michael Shapiro

Chapter 12:
NEW SOCIAL RELATIONSHIPS

In the mid-'60s and early '70s, the neighborhood became much more diverse but still remained very segregated. African American families occupied the area from Boston Road south and east to Prospect Avenue and the area surrounding Morris High School. Latinos, principally Puerto Rican families, occupied the area west of Claremont Parkway to Webster Avenue. The atmosphere in the neighborhood reflected these changes. Stores, bodegas, and soul food replaced small European groceries and butchers. Each ethnic and nationality group claimed ownership of its own terrain. Most stayed within their own areas of security, which were defined by housing, church and school. However, tensions existed. The community could be described as a melting pot, but it was hardly harmonious or integrated. The public school was the integrative assembly, but even it had limits and fostered self-segregating. The contact between ethnic groups was restricted and, at times, hostile. The Jewish, Italian, and Irish groups were now clearly threatened by the newcomers. Few institutions existed that could integrate the changes in both demographics and geography. Two of the community centers that attempted to provide some programs in intergroup relations were Bronx House and the East Bronx Y. Unfortunately, funding became problematic for both organizations, and they abandoned the neighborhood for more affluent communities.

The park was a sought-after respite from an otherwise high-density tenement existence. The people who lived around the park on all four sides jealously guarded their rights to stay and protect their turf. The old-timers would say of the newcomers, "They may be here, but they're not going to take over our park." Youth were influenced by this attitude and there was a fearful atmosphere that sometimes led to fights and skirmishes whenever large numbers of African American teens or Latino gangs were in the park. These were short-lived but strangely exciting and led to stories of great exaggeration. No weapons were ever used and the skirmishes were often centered on "potato wars"— throwing potatoes or eggs at each other with occasional fistfights. While intergroup tensions were triggered by confrontations, there was no fear of drive-by shootings or any serious injury as a result of the changing neighborhood population as is the case today. Geoff Canada's book *Fist, Stick, Knife, Gun*, written in the mid-'90s, reflects a very different normative behavior. The fist was replaced by the stick, which was replaced by the knife, and then the gun. Fatality was a common occurrence in the '70s, '80s, and early '90s, which was not the case in earlier years.

One major policy change had a very significant positive outcome. In the 1950s the board of education rezoned the neighborhood high school so that white, black, and Latino students all had to attend Morris High School. Prior to that decision, Morris had almost exclusively African American students, while James Monroe and Taft high schools were made up of white students only. There was an outcry on the part of white parents about the decision, but over time it was accepted. Morris became one of the few integrated high schools in New York City. Apprehension eventually grew into some understanding and relationships between different races. White and black students not only shared classes but were also on the basketball varsity team or baseball squad with Puerto Rican students. This "arrangement" had a social and political effect on the environment. Friday-night dances were integrated and social clubs were formed. Groups of diverse students worked and walked together. It was a remarkable experience, and those who attended Morris High School were the early beneficiaries of an integrated environment. Turfs began to break down, parental attitudes became more tolerant, and social relations among young people became significantly more progressive. The block was becoming less secular and insular and more a part of the larger community. Several members of the group became identified with social causes that addressed larger issues of a racial or ethnic nature. Several of the block residents became involved and active in civil rights organizations and persuaded some of the other members of the block to become interested and curious about these new social movements.

I have often tried to recount the steps and the twists and turns of my own adolescence, especially during my high school years. While I became a good student who was inquisitive, I have often wondered why I pursued social causes that took me away from my core group of friends and consumed me with a sense of societal injustice and later on, activism. Those issues, fighting against the war machine and for minority rights, equality, and fairness were so compelling that I was willing to give up the security of my block relationships and branch out with new friendships and a different lifestyle. I was intensively involved in left-of-center organizations because they were best able to effect the changes that reflected my beliefs.

What propelled me and not some of my peers to move in that direction? Why was I willing to risk social ostracism in order to fulfill what I believed was now at the core of my existence? These social causes transcended academic achievement, peer relationships, and even family obligations. The power of a cause, a direction, a sense of group solidarity, a union of believers became the most important elements of my life. I am certain that these factors are what led me to become a social worker. Each member of the block community found his or her own direction, be it engineering, law, teaching, or higher education and developed new primary groups and civic, religious, or spiritual connections. My belief, however, is that our experiences on the block, our deep friendship, our shared experience, our sense of trust in one another, our working-class orientation, our inventiveness—and in some ways our disdain for authority—were a central motivation that permitted each of us to find his or her own direction. As it is said, "Fear often trumps logic," but social cause and commitment have the power to overcome fear.

Teaching Questions

A. How is group solidarity an important step in the creation of a substitute family?

B. How can leadership create a new social environment?

C. How do community organization skills help to bring people together and create a new social force?

D. How can social workers and community organizers serve constituents and clients to resolve social and ethnic tension?

E. What should the role of the community centers and settlement houses be in creating a new social milieu?

F. What role should the public high school play as a positive force for change?

Selected Readings:

- *Manual for Intergroup Relations* by John P. Dean, Alex Rosen

- *Organization Practice*, Second Edition by Mary Katherine O' Connor and F. Ellen Netting: pages 153 - 239

- *The Challenge of Change: Leadership Strategies for Not-for-Profit Executives and Boards* by Philip Coltoff: pages 45 - 73

- *Confidentiality and Social Work* by Suanna J. Wilson

Chapter 13:
IDEAS, IDEOLOGY, AND SELF-CONCEPT

What happened to the young people living on the block? How was their growth impacted by their experiences as block members, and how were those experiences then integrated into the fabric of their personalities? Considering all of the factors that determine growth, did their lives on the block change their future direction? One of the ways to examine impact is to reach for feelings that often lie beneath the surface. Did the definitions imposed by the block's social network help to define its young residents' future sense of self and group standing? For example, did Hymie who was a poor athlete, chubby, unattractive to girls, and a follower in group life, change his self-definition as he moved away from the block and into life's other circles? Did the leaders continue to exhibit leadership? Was their sense of self so secure and developed that they exercised those same qualities in young adulthood and adulthood? What happened on the block to shape the values, sense of self, and definition of accomplishment that remained a part of their personalities?

Some of these questions are best answered by the participants themselves. I have located several of them and asked that they not only respond to questionnaires but also write an essay about what the block meant to them and what they have carried forth from those experiences that impacted their lives. Did the group members experience the same sense of togetherness? How did they feel about the roles assigned to them? Did the working-class nature of the block provide a platform for later political thinking and ideology? Did family life and intercultural experiences affect one's sense of others?

It's fascinating to think about how our early experiences, particularly those during our developmental years, affected us as we become more independent and productive members of society. Other than family the block was the social instrument that defined each of its inhabitants and provided them with a footprint for the future.

Teaching Questions

A. In what ways does a social ideology develop?

B. Do peer group experiences influence self-concept?

C. What are the early experiences that serve as positive forces for healthy social and emotional development?

D. Why does nostalgia influence present and future thinking?

Selected Readings:

- *Theories for Direct Social Work Practice* by Joseph Walsh: pages 80 - 102, 107 - 128, 182 - 190

- *Delinquency and Opportunity: A Theory of Delinquent Gangs* by Richard A. Cloward and Lloyd E. Ohlin

- *The Child Savers: Juvenile Justice Observed* by Peter S. Prescott

- *Rachel and Her Children: Homeless Families in America* by Jonathan Kozol

- *The Small Group* by Michael S. Olmstead, published by Smith College/Random House

Chapter 14:
RECOLLECTIONS IN THEIR OWN WORDS

Gerald Harris:

There was an ever-present tension on the block between appreciation of education—as preached by immigrant mothers—and a perceived need to be tough and athletic—as taught by the streets of the South Bronx. Success in school might well please the folks, but it risked the ridicule of one's peers. You could skip class and maybe get away with it; but you could never duck a fight unless you were prepared to go into hiding.

This tug-of-war came to a head one day when a dispute erupted between the smart kids and the tough guys. The fight was set for 3:30 in the playground across from the school. It was the "jocks" against the "fags." I was a jock; but if everything was stripped away, I worried which side would claim me. I liked to run, but I loved to read. I could catch and throw with the best but shivered with awe in the presence of Egyptian relics at the museum. I used "fuck" as an adjective and wrote poetry on the bathroom wall. I never knew for sure whether its preservation reflected my mother's admiration or her lack of good housekeeping.

Now, you understand, fag wasn't used to describe a sexual preference. The term referred to those who did their homework, got good grades, and valued intellect over brawn. They were the first chosen to recite, the last taken in "choose up."

I valued my distinction as a jock; but at some level I suspected that the fags would ultimately get the high-paying jobs and, therefore, the beautiful women. Still, until adult standards became a measuring stick, it was important for me to maintain my then peer-favored status.

This meant that at times I would behave clownishly in class, neglect homework, and make myself a general pain in the ass to the beleaguered teachers. My conduct drew the grades it merited and so my reputation as a not very good student was secure.

When senior year arrived and the issue became whether I had grades that permitted admission to a tuition-free city college, I decided to get serious. The result, the highest grade in each academic subject, so stunned my homeroom teacher that he asked to see the graded exam papers. Finally, he capitulated to the notion that I might actually be smarter than he had assumed.

He asked me to stay after class and said: "I was about to give you a failing grade in citizenship and deportment. However, far be it for me to ruin such an outstanding report card. So, I am giving you an A in those categories." So my grades effectively made me a model citizen notwithstanding my boorish behavior. I knew there was a life lesson to be learned in this scenario.

Oh, the fight. It took place as scheduled. I never threw a punch. Instead, I pulled aside the best philosophy student in the class and discussed the meaning of Descartes' "I think, therefore I am," as we feigned striking blows.

Old Neighborhood Recollections

By Peter Lerner

It was our universe. It was an environment in which we grew and thrived. Our neighborhood was stable with little turnover. It was a very desirable place to live for a working-class population.

Our neighborhood was part of the East Bronx (now generally referred to as the South Bronx). It stretched from Crotona Avenue in the south to Crotona Park North. The most compelling feature of the neighborhood was the park: Crotona Park. The park was a natural extension of our block—Crotona Park East, which we referred to as C.P.E. The 188-acre park was the focal point. It offered many opportunities for kids and adults alike: ball fields, basketball courts, tennis courts, handball courts, playgrounds, a swimming pool, a lake, and even bocce courts.

As kids we were consumed with sports and street games of all kinds. We played with passion and enthusiasm every day until dark or into the night. We often played until our parents called us in for meals. Our immigrant parents, who had different values from us American-born kids, thought sports and games were a waste of time.

We played all the major sports with inferior or little equipment. We played with baseballs until the covers tore off. Then we used adhesive tape to make new covers. When our bats broke, we nailed them back together and played on. We saved our money for special purchases. There was no instant gratification on our block!

We played pickup games and chose sides without adult supervision. We didn't wait to be driven to activities. We traveled by bus and subway ourselves, and our parents didn't own cars anyway. We wore sneakers for their utility, not as a fashion statement. We wore baseball hats only when we played baseball. We enjoyed every activity the park offered except tennis, but we were amused by the people in funny white outfits who flocked to the tennis courts. (Today, those courts are the site of an annual professional tournament.)

Crotona Park served as a sanctuary during heat waves. Nobody had air-conditioning, so on hot summer nights some residents slept in the park or on fire escapes. Fear of crime didn't exist.

Park benches, of which there were many, and building stoops played a very important role in community life. Especially at night, everyone would gather there for lively discussions of anything and everything! Stoops, at the entrances to the apartment buildings, were introduced to New Amsterdam by the Dutch in early colonial times. Then, too, residents congregated to exchange tidbits.

Stoops served another important purpose. We played a game called off the point, in which a spaldeen was thrown against the point of a stoop step acting as a bat. The word "spaldeen" was a perversion of "Spaulding," the name of the company that manufactured the rubber ball. The bases were run in the usual manner, with the street serving as the infield, while the defenders tried to record an out.

In April 1945, after watching *Gone with the Wind* at the Boston, I noticed small groups of adults clustered on the streets. They told me that FDR had died. This made a huge impression on me, as I knew that my parents and the whole neighborhood loved him.

Radio was another source of entertainment. We faithfully listened to *The Shadow*, *Captain Midnight*, and *The Lone Ranger*. Older kids favored *Martin Block* and the *Make-Believe Ballroom*, which featured the top hits and Block's popular sign-off, "Good night to you and you and especially to you." It never ceases to amaze me that radio's popularity lasted for fewer than thirty years!

Adults on the block enjoyed "playing the numbers," a cheap and popular form of gambling. Players would bet on a three-digit number of their choice. The winning number was determined by sources that the promoters of the game could not control, such as bank financial balances or pari-mutuels totals at racetracks.

Gambling of all sorts was very popular. As an eleven-year-old, I was a runner who collected football betting slips for a neighborhood bookmaker, or "bookie." I remember being especially excited when I had betting slips in my pockets and the police cruised by. Card playing was another favorite pastime for kids and adults. We played poker, casino, knuckles (or, as we called it, knucks), rummy, and "steal the old man's bundle."

Losing at knucks could be painful: the loser's knuckles were hit hard with the edge of a deck of cards; the blows sometimes drew blood.

Unions and Politics

Voters on the block mostly supported Democratic Party candidates. The American Labor Party, which existed primarily in New York State, was to the left of the Democratic Party but usually endorsed Democratic candidates. My father voted on the ALP line because he was encouraged to do so by the painters union, to which he belonged. The Republican Party was thought of as the party of the rich. It was hard to find Republicans anywhere in our neighborhood.

Most workers were union members who support-ed New Deal legislation such as Social Security and the National Labor Relations Act, which guaranteed union rights. They felt that unions provided the means for upward mobility, which they sought for their families. Many people in the neighborhood worked in the garment indus-try. They brought skills valuable in the "needle trades" with them to America when they arrived from Europe. They were garment cutters, pressers, and pattern makers and were usually members of the ILGWU, the International Ladies Garment Workers Union, one of the largest and most powerful unions in New York City.

May Day, May 1, was set aside to honor working people. New York City's annual May Day parade in Manhattan's Union Square brought out thousands of workers, particularly from unions with Socialist leanings. Their members marched enthusiastically to support pro-union legislation. Members of my family and our neighbors marched in these parades every year.

My first job during high school was to work part time as a stock boy for a small dress company in Manhattan's garment district. As I made deliveries, I often pushed heavy racks of clothes through the teeming streets of the district. My later involvement in the UFT, New York City's teachers' union, stemmed from my early working experiences and my parents' union loyalties.

The Candy Store

The candy store occupied a special place in our neighborhood. Every neighborhood had at least one; ours had two, located across the street from each other. Our loyalties shifted between the two.

The candy store was much more than a place to buy candy. It was a place for gossip, heated sports arguments, and, for our fathers, discussions of the war's progress. It was also a place to hear music on the jukebox. In winter, the candy store's air was heavy with cigarette and cigar smoke. Candy store favorites were egg creams (no egg, no cream, just milk, seltzer, and chocolate syrup) and glasses of "two-cent plain," otherwise known as seltzer.

The Bronx

Louise Patalano Wszulkowski

What was it like growing up in the East Bronx? For me, having moved from a small New England town in 1943 to Wilkins Avenue and Crotona Park East, it was both exciting and scary. The neighborhood seemed vast, with many large tenements and stores, buses and trolleys, and people everywhere. Certainly our main street in New Hampshire couldn't compare to this new place.

I was enrolled in P.S. 61 with Miss Gotlieb as my first grade teacher. I quickly made many school friends and slowly felt more secure and at home in my new neighborhood. I have wonderful recollections of P.S. 61, having loved my many teachers. And then there was Mary, an Italian janitor at the school. Mary befriended my mom and therefore became the recipient of many of Mom's pizziola sandwiches, which were kept warm on the classroom radiator. Ahhh, the aroma filled the air. I also remember a sweet old gentleman who sold sticks of sliced apples and prunes dipped in a warm glaze for three cents each during recess and after school. Yummy!

Soon we graduated from public school and moved on to junior high and ninth grade. Herman Ridder (P.S. 98) was the BEST! I remember Dr. Gillis's English class. Mary B. Gillis gave a stern appearance and although some considered her too strict, I thought she was a helluva good teacher. In her class I found a love for Greek mythology and English in general.

Another person I remember well was my Spanish teacher, Mrs. Diaz. I can still recite "Henny Penny" in Spanish. Thank you, Mrs. Diaz.

Our neighborhood was a mix of Jewish, Irish, Italian, and Spanish families. We all lived very peacefully in this Crotona Park neighborhood. I learned about (and to this day love) lox and cream cheese, gefilte fish, matzo balls, and borscht. Mrs. Stein, our next-door neighbor and good friend, kept a strict kosher home. Nonetheless, when Mrs. Patalano was cooking a pot of spaghetti sauce and meatballs, Mrs. Stein presented herself for a "snack."

Sam Yokel and his cousin Izzy ran the neighborhood grocery store. A quarter pound of butter was cut from a large chunk in the refrigerator—no tubs or sticks for Sam! Cream cheese was sold by the pound from a wooden container, and you could buy single eggs if you wished. There were bagels, rolls, and lox aplenty.

Next to Yokel's grocery was the kosher butcher shop, and around the corner on Wilkins Avenue was Mr. Wing's Chinese laundry. Mr. and Mrs. Wing had five daughters and were a very lovely family. The Greek shoemaker and his wife ran their shoe shop. No gluing of shoes here. All the work was done to perfection by hand and with large mending machines. I can still remember the scent of leather and polish that greeted us each time we stepped inside.

One of our favorite haunts was Nemeroff's candy store on the corner of Wilkins and Crotona Park. All of our crew hung out at the candy store whenever we could. Counters were stocked with chocolate marshmallow twists, candy button strips, chocolate jelly rounds, chocolate licorice, tootsie pops, and more. Malted milks, egg creams, ice cream sodas, and lemon-lime rickies were favorites. Don't forget the two-cents plains! Best of all were the chocolate mellow rolls from Horton's Ice Cream Company. We had many great times at Nemeroff's. Etched in my memory is "Jerry" the candy store bookie, who always had a wisecrack to share. The phone booth in the candy store received many a phone call for the Patalano family. Someone would buzz our apartment (#11) at 1567 Wilkins and inform us of a call. It cost only a nickel to make a phone call at that time. Imagine that.

Directly across Wilkins and Crotona was Sol's candy store. This was a gathering place for the "older guys." It was the same situation, the boys and girls flirting, listening to music, and hanging out.

Summertime was my favorite time of year. We filled our days playing jacks and ball on the stoop or jumping double-dutch on the sidewalks. There were craft programs in the park and walks around Indian Lake. The boys pitched pennies. A game of stoop ball or stickball was played on many a day.

Summertime also brought sunbathing on tar beach. A mixture of baby oil and iodine was slathered on our bathing-suit-clad bodies while we listened to the latest songs on our radios. Bungalow Bar Ice Cream Delights cruised the park daily—my favorites were burnt almond or coconut ice cream bars or the old standby, chocolate or strawberry sundaes. Warm nights were spent sitting on the park benches waiting for the guys to join us. We would hash out the day's events and plan our next get-together. We could peacefully sit on the park benches until late evening without any fear of danger. When babysitting, we invited the guys and girls over for snacks, dancing to records and smooching. Nat King Cole's "Too Young" was one of my favorites.

Not only was I involved with many friends in this close neighborhood, I was also surrounded by loving relatives. My paternal grandparents lived on this block as well as aunts, uncles, and cousins. I was sure to have family looking out for my sister and me.

These are but a few of my memories of this wonderful Bronx neighborhood in which I was privileged to spend much of my youth. From this time in my life I learned the importance of friendship, strong family ties, and the ease of befriending people with different backgrounds and customs. Neighborhoods like Crotona Park are fewer today, but it remains very vivid in my mind and will always bring a smile to my face.

Happy Days
By Anthony Scotti

Phil asked me to write down some of my recollections and thoughts about the five guys (the Big Five) who made up the inner circle of our friendship and how we got together. The inner circle started out of necessity, since we entered a period of our youth when we were undergoing a series of experiences that were major challenges for each of us. As we faced a new independence, our security blanket was temporarily lost. We learned to begin to rely on each other as a replacement for the comfort of family.

The five of us were very fortunate for the friendship and closeness that emerged and we were the products of an era, an environment; a neighborhood that offered the collective support of our friends, siblings, neighbors, and parents. We also were the recipients of the major investment of Franklin Delano Roosevelt's New Deal—public-service programs that enriched our lives.

The strong bond and love that I will always retain for my guys started in kindergarten, when we independently navigated our daily journey to P.S. 61, and then through elementary school, junior high school, adolescence, and young adulthood. I attended Stewie's, Gerald's, and Phil's bar mitzvahs, and they attended Lou's and my confirmations. While our talents were first being developed, we demonstrated an interest in building projects, from our clubhouse to scooters and wagons. These projects took a great amount of time to plan and develop, including finding creative methods to implement the logistics and challenges of obtaining materials leading up to the actual construction.

As time passed, it became clear that Gerry would excel in school; Phil would become our political activist; Stewie our musical talent and comic, and Lou and I our engineers.

It has been a great ride, and Stewie was wrong when he said my first date to the junior high dance smelled like glue and predicted my wife would be short, fat, with a gold tooth and wear her hair in a bun.

Phil Coltoff

I have often looked back in my internal rearview mirror to assess those critical adolescent years and to determine their effect on my development. The block was a place of such innocence, experimentation, and youthful joy that over the years I have been moved to revisit it, the park, and the school many times. The friendships and the intimacies shared between boys (and, later, girls) were such that they carry great meaning that goes beyond nostalgia. I believe that these relationships were the models that I used for the development of further adult relationships. What was it like to share feelings and experience joy together—a victory in a ball game; hatching a plan for a new adventure, like a bike trip to the Palisades in New Jersey; a trip to Orchard Beach unaccompanied by your parents; or hitchhiking to the Catskill Mountains? All of these events contributed to my sense of who I was as a person, who I could count on, and, in small ways, what I would become.

As our urban society has grown more complex, I am saddened that blocks, while still existing as a physical entity, most often do not have the social/emotional connections that they had in the past. Families don't know each other as they once did; neighbors often live isolated, and at times, alienated lives; and children do not have, as Collin Powell has said, "the Aunties" that were the block lookouts. I believe that the block I describe in this book was a social safety net that allowed families of all ethnicities and persuasions to share a community together, accept one another, and accept their differences in doing so. Families were sustained because they were supported and reinforced by their neighbors and by the block culture.

Our peers formed a circle that, as Erik Erikson has written in his eight stages of man, allowed for autonomy and identity and minimized shame, doubt, and role confusion. There was a predictability that centered on the relationships among the youth that provided a blanket of security and reduced uncertainty and fear. Social work agencies, such as settlement houses, community centers, and public schools, need to restate their function; better understand the nature of group life; become, once again, block-oriented, and be committed to social justice. I believe this can help to reestablish a lost sense of community.

For me, the block was the stepping-stone, the benchmark. Morris High School was my experimental laboratory, and the neighborhood was my political arena. I became a left-winger, today referred to as a "progressive," who believed in the rights of all people to a better life and more active political representation. My future was sealed, even though I did not recognize it at the time. I would become an activist, a person who would put his ideas and, at times, his being in the forefront for human rights.

I owe much to the block, its people, its culture, its friendships, and its own unique safety net. My own path took me to summer camp as a counselor; a part-time club leader in a local settlement house; a youth board street club worker (after college); a social worker as part of the first major delinquency prevention program in the nation; a mental health counselor; a program director, and, ultimately, the executive director and CEO of the Children's Aid Society (one of the largest youth and family organizations serving nonprofits in our country). After twenty-five years as the head of this organization, I partially retired and embarked on an encore career as a visiting professor and executive-in-residence at the New York University Silver School of Social Work. My fate had been cast many years earlier.

Notes: